CHILDREN'S ILLUSTRATORS

JERRY PINKNEY

Sheila Griffin Llanas
ABDO Publishing Company

visit us at
www.abdopublishing.com

Published by ABDO Publishing Company, PO Box 398166, Minneapolis, MN 55439. Copyright © 2012 by Abdo Consulting Group, Inc. International copyrights reserved in all countries. No part of this book may be reproduced in any form without written permission from the publisher. The Checkerboard Library™ is a trademark and logo of ABDO Publishing Company.

Printed in the United States of America, North Mankato, Minnesota.
102011
012012

 PRINTED ON RECYCLED PAPER

Cover Photo: Courtesy Jerry Pinkney. Photograph by Thomas Kristich. All rights reserved. Used with permission.
Interior Photos: AP Images p. 5; courtesy Curtis Compton / American Library Association / www.ala.org p. 18; Corbis p. 16; iBerkshires.com / Nichole Dupont p. 15; iStockphoto p. 6; courtesy Jeffrey Malet p. 9; Ron Tarver, MCT/Landov p. 11; From USA Today, February 5, 2010 © 2010 USA Today. All rights reserved. Used by permission and protected by the Copyright Laws of the United States. The printing, copying, redistribution, or retransmission of this Content without express written permission is prohibited. p. 12
The Talking Eggs by Robert D. San Souci and Jerry Pinkney. Used by permission of Penguin Group (USA) Inc. All rights reserved. p. 7
The Patchwork Quilt by Valerie Flournoy and Jerry Pinkney. Used by permission of Penguin Group (USA) Inc. All rights reserved. p. 14
The Moon Over Star by Dianna Hutts Aston and Jerry Pinkney. Used by permission of Penguin Group (USA) Inc. All rights reserved. p. 17
The Lion and the Mouse by Jerry Pinkney. Reprinted by permission of Little Brown and Company, a division of Hachette Book Group, Inc. p. 19
Three Little Kittens by Jerry Pinkney. Used by permission of Penguin Group (USA) Inc. All rights reserved. p. 20

Series Coordinator: BreAnn Rumsch / Editors: Megan M. Gunderson, BreAnn Rumsch
Art Direction: Neil Klinepier

Library of Congress Cataloging-in-Publication Data

Llanas, Sheila Griffin, 1958-
 Jerry Pinkney / Sheila Griffin Llanas.
    p. cm. -- (Children's illustrators)
 Includes index.
 ISBN 978-1-61783-247-5
 1. Pinkney, Jerry--Juvenile literature. 2. Illustrators--United States--Biography--Juvenile literature. I. Pinkney, Jerry. II. Title.
 NC975.5.P56L59 2012
 741.6'42--dc23
                              2011030113

CONTENTS

LIFELONG STORYTELLER

Jerry Pinkney's first picture book appeared in 1964. Today, more than 100 books have his name on their covers. Over the years, he has received dozens of awards for his work. He has won five **Coretta Scott King Awards** and illustrated five **Caldecott Honor Books**. And at age 70, Pinkney won the Caldecott Medal.

In addition to picture books, Pinkney has created art for National Geographic, the US Postal Service, NASA, and the White House. He also has had 30 art exhibitions at museums such as the Art Institute of Chicago in Illinois and the Norman Rockwell Museum in Stockbridge, Massachusetts.

As a young man, Pinkney wanted to express his African-American **heritage** and **culture**. He was determined to be a strong **role model** for his family and community. Today, readers young and old consider Pinkney a national treasure.

Through his art, Pinkney (second from left) is one of today's master storytellers.

PHILADELPHIA CHILDHOOD

Jerry Pinkney was born in Philadelphia, Pennsylvania, on December 22, 1939. He was the fourth of James and

Downtown Philadelphia

Williemae Pinkney's six children. Jerry had two brothers and three sisters. The family lived in a small house in a tight-knit African-American community.

Philadelphia is a city with many **cultures**. Jewish and Italian families lived one block over on either side of Jerry's Germantown street. So early on, Jerry was aware of other cultures and races.

Jerry's parents had come to Philadelphia from the South. James was a jack-of-all-trades. He earned his living as a plumber, electrician, and carpenter. Williemae took care of the home and children.

As an adult, Pinkney included his uncle's pony in **The Talking Eggs, *a Creole folktale.***

Williemae often read to her children and told them stories in the Southern **oral tradition**. She entertained them with the legend of John Henry and tales of Uncle Remus. Jerry especially loved to hear Aesop's fables, such as "The Lion and the Mouse."

After all, Jerry was fascinated by animals. In Philadelphia, he enjoyed trips to the city zoo. And when his family visited relatives outside the city and in the New Jersey countryside, he got to see animals in nature. One uncle even had a pony!

Jerry loved those weekends away. The children played outside, swam, and explored the woods. For young Jerry, life was a great adventure.

ART AND ACADEMICS

At home, the Pinkneys had no television. But the children were never bored. They had paper and pencils for drawing. And, James often brought home wallpaper scraps for them to use in art projects.

Jerry's older brothers loved to draw, and Jerry followed their example. It wasn't long before the Pinkneys noticed that Jerry was the artist of the family.

Jerry's talent was also noted at school. Growing up, he attended Hill Elementary School. In first grade, he drew a fire engine on the blackboard. His teacher and classmates praised his work. From then on, Jerry was known as the class artist.

Eager to learn, Jerry tried his best. He **excelled** at art. But reading was a real struggle for him. And spelling was almost impossible. No one knew at the time, but Jerry had **dyslexia**. In the 1940s, teachers had little information about learning disorders. So, they could not help Jerry.

Jerry had to help himself. Drawing built his **confidence** and helped him focus on his studies. In spite of his learning challenge, Jerry's determination helped him earn excellent grades.

As a child, drawing helped Jerry feel calm and happy. He feels great satisfaction to be able to make art every day for his job.

FROM ART TO ARTIST

After elementary school, Jerry attended Roosevelt Junior High. Unfortunately, the school did not offer many art classes. So, Jerry took private art lessons. He carried a sketchbook with him everywhere.

At age 12, Jerry got a job at a newsstand. When he was not busy selling newspapers, Jerry drew in his sketchbook. He often drew people walking by or waiting for the bus.

One day, a customer saw Jerry's art. It was cartoonist John Liney. He drew the popular comic strip *Henry*. Mr. Liney invited Jerry to visit his art studio a few blocks away.

Jerry was amazed by the big drawing table and all the art supplies. He had never met a professional artist before. The experience was eye-opening for Jerry. He realized art did not have to be a hobby. It could be a real job!

Jerry attended Dobbins Vocational High School. There, he studied commercial art. At a Valentine's sweetheart dance, he met a fellow student named Gloria Jean Maultsby. For the young couple, it was "like at first sight." Gloria admired Jerry's determination. At just 16, Jerry already knew exactly what he wanted to do with his life.

Today, Pinkney works in his own large, airy studio. It is full of art supplies, much like Mr. Liney's was!

TAKING A STAND

The Pinkney family is close. And many creative family members contribute to children's books!

Pinkney graduated from high school in 1957. Then, he became the first in his family to attend college. Pinkney had earned a full **scholarship** to the Philadelphia Museum College of Art. There, he loved taking classes in printmaking and painting.

Pinkney married Gloria in 1960, and they soon started a family. Eventually they had four children. Their daughter is named Troy Bernadette. Their sons are named Scott Cannon, Jerry Brian, and Myles Carter.

Before Pinkney could complete college, the young family moved to Boston, Massachusetts. At first, Pinkney worked as a florist. Then he found a job at the Rustcraft Greeting Card Company. There, he learned all he could about design and printing.

At the time, many people in Boston were interested in the **civil rights movement**. Pinkney saw the need for this fight to include books. He found few books about African-American history and **culture** for his children to read. Pinkney wanted to change that.

In 1964, Pinkney illustrated his first book. It was *The Adventures of Spider: West African Folktales*, retold by Joyce Cooper Arkhurst. This project showed Pinkney his passion was for making **multicultural** children's books.

GROWING RECOGNITION

Over time, Pinkney worked on more children's books. As an illustrator, he merged his art skills with his **heritage**. So, Pinkney's early books retell African and African-American folktales. They include *More Adventures of Spider*, *Femi and Old Grandaddie*, and *Song of the Trees*.

Meanwhile, Pinkney had been working in different art studios. Then, the Pinkney family moved to Croton-on-Hudson, New York. There, Pinkney opened the Jerry Pinkney Studio in 1971. He designed textbooks and advertisements for this business.

During the next 14 years, Pinkney illustrated dozens of children's books. Then in 1985, *The Patchwork Quilt* by Valerie

Flournoy was published. Pinkney had painted a loving African-American grandmother and granddaughter for the book. The next year, the book earned Pinkney his first **Coretta Scott King Illustrator Award**.

Pinkney's success meant he could now focus on picture books. One project was *Mirandy and Brother Wind* by Patricia C. McKissack. Pinkney's watercolor paintings show Mirandy trying to get Brother Wind to help her win a **cakewalk**. In 1989, the book won the first of Pinkney's **Caldecott Honors**. It also earned a Coretta Scott King Illustrator Award.

Pinkney has won the Coretta Scott King Illustrator Award more times than any other illustrator.

WINNING STYLE

Pinkney's career continued to develop. In 1995, Julius Lester retold the folktale *John Henry*. Pinkney loved painting the story's larger than life African-American hero. Two years later, Pinkney imagined life as a slave child on an 1820s plantation. His art illustrated *Minty: A Story of Young Harriet Tubman* by Alan Schroeder.

In 2002, Pinkney won his fifth **Coretta Scott King Illustrator Award** for McKissack's *Goin' Someplace Special*. The next year, he **adapted** and illustrated *Noah's Ark*. The book earned his fifth **Caldecott Honor**. And in 2009, Pinkney won his fourth Coretta Scott King Illustrator

Whether in children's books or for historical works, Pinkney brings the African-American spirit to life in his art.

Honor Award for *The Moon Over Star* written by Dianna Hutts Aston.

Pinkney works on his illustrations in his bright studio. There is no phone or computer there. But music can be heard playing during the day. Pinkney prefers classical in the morning and jazz in the afternoon.

When Pinkney starts a new project, he begins with a lot of research. He often works with models, too. Family members sometimes wear costumes

and create different poses. Pinkney then takes their pictures. Later, these help him create realistic images.

Next, Pinkney begins working on the art. He starts by making **thumbnail** sketches. For the final paintings, he draws with pencil and adds watercolor with delicate brushstrokes. The tiny details form big pictures that shimmer with life. On average, it takes Pinkney about six months to finish the art for one book.

No Words Needed

Pinkney had been illustrating for almost 50 years when he got an idea for a new book. He wanted to illustrate an Aesop's fable. It was an old favorite that he remembered well from his childhood, "The Lion and the Mouse."

In the tale, a lion spares a mouse's life. In return, the mouse saves the lion from hunters. Pinkney says he loves the fable because "both animals are equally large at heart."

Pinkney is still fascinated by animals, just like he was as a child. So, many of his books feature creatures flying, running,

The Lion and the Mouse *was published in 2009.*

ELEMENTS OF ART: TONE

Tone is one of the basic parts of art. It is the level of color in an art piece. Tone can be deep, pale, or anywhere in between.

Pinkney prefers to draw his illustrations with pencil and then paint them with watercolors. Up close, you can see the detailed pattern of his countless brushstrokes. Pinkney builds the tones of his colors in layers, creating the effects of light and shadow. This helps his images look more realistic from far away.

or swimming. Because animals cannot speak, Pinkney gives them vivid facial expressions. This was especially important in *The Lion and the Mouse*.

Pinkney started drawing the story's pictures, planning to add the text later. But then he made a book **dummy** and paged through it. He realized his pictures already told the whole story! So he did not have to add words.

Pinkney knew *The Lion and the Mouse* was special. And indeed it was. On the morning of January 18, 2010, Pinkney got an exciting phone call. He had won the **Caldecott Medal** for *The Lion and the Mouse*!

That day happened to be Martin Luther King Day. Significantly, this was also the first time an individual African American had earned the award.

Since that proud moment, Pinkney has continued to make more wonderful books. He **adapted** and illustrated *Three Little Kittens* in 2010. Then, he got to work adapting the famous children's lullaby for *Twinkle, Twinkle, Little Star*. This beautiful book was published in 2011.

Looking back on Pinkney's career, the list of his awards is long. He has devoted his life to expressing his African-American roots through his art. And, he never let **dyslexia** slow him down.

WINNING TITLES

Jerry Pinkney is among today's most honored children's book creators. Check out his top award winners, including those named Caldecott Honor Books (CHB) and Coretta Scott King Illustrator (CSKI) Awards and Honor Awards. How many have you read?

BOOK TITLE, AUTHOR	AWARD(S), YEAR WON
The Patchwork Quilt, by Valerie Flournoy	CSKI Award, 1986
Half a Moon and One Whole Star, by Crescent Dragonwagon	CSKI Award, 1987
Mirandy and Brother Wind, by Patricia C. McKissack	CHB & CSKI Award, 1989
The Talking Eggs, by Robert D. San Souci	CHB & CSKI Honor Award, 1990
John Henry, by Julius Lester	CHB, 1995
Minty: A Story of Young Harriet Tubman, by Alan Schroeder	CSKI Award, 1997
The Ugly Duckling, by Jerry Pinkney	CHB, 2000
Goin' Someplace Special, by Patricia C. McKissack	CSKI Award, 2002
Noah's Ark, by Jerry Pinkney	CHB, 2003
God Bless the Child, by Billie Holiday	CSKI Honor Award, 2005
The Moon Over Star, by Dianna Hutts Aston	CSKI Honor Award, 2009
The Lion and the Mouse, by Jerry Pinkney	Caldecott Medal, 2010

Today Pinkney loves reading, **adapting** folktales, teaching art, and helping children. But mostly, he loves to paint. He says his favorite project is always the one on his drawing table. Pinkney set high goals for himself as a young man. Through passion and determination, he achieved every one of them.

GLOSSARY

adapt - to change a story for presenting in another form.

cakewalk - an African-American activity in which a cake is the prize for the most accomplished steps and figures in walking.

Caldecott Honor Book - a runner-up to the Caldecott Medal. The Caldecott Medal is an award the American Library Association gives to the artist who illustrated the year's best picture book.

civil rights movement - a movement in the United States in the 1950s and 1960s. It consisted of organized efforts to end laws that involved unequal treatment of African Americans.

confidence - faith in oneself and one's powers.

Coretta Scott King Award - an annual award given by the American Library Association. It honors African-American authors and illustrators whose work reflects the African-American experience. Runners-up are called honor books.

culture - the customs, arts, and tools of a nation or a people at a certain time. Something related to culture is cultural.

dummy - a manuscript laid out in book form, with sketches and finished samples of all the illustrations.

dyslexia - a condition in the brain that makes it hard for a person to read, write, and spell.

excel - to be better than others.

heritage - something handed down from one generation to the next.

multicultural - of, relating to, or blending different cultures.

oral tradition - the traditional knowledge of a culture passed through verbal communication. It consists of stories, poems, songs, myths, dramas, rituals, proverbs, and riddles.

role model - a person whose behavior serves as a standard for others to follow.

scholarship - money or aid given to help a student continue his or her studies.

thumbnail - a small, rough sketch drawn by an artist before he or she makes the full-sized sketch.

WEB SITES

To learn more about Jerry Pinkney, visit ABDO Publishing Company online. Web sites about Jerry Pinkney are featured on our Book Links page. These links are routinely monitored and updated to provide the most current information available.
www.abdopublishing.com

INDEX

Your

Travel

Guide to

ANCIENT
CHINA

Your Travel Guide to
ANCIENT CHINA

Josepha Sherman

↳ LERNER PUBLICATIONS COMPANY • MINNEAPOLIS

Lerner Publications Company
A division of Lerner Publishing Group
241 First Avenue North
Minneapolis, MN 55401 U.S.A.

Website address: www.lernerbooks.com

Library of Congress Cataloging-in-Publication Data

Sherman, Josepha.
    Your travel guide to ancient China / by Josepha Sherman.
      p.   cm. — (Passport to history)
    Audience: "Age 10–14."
    Summary: Takes readers on a journey back in time in order to experience life in China during the Han Dynasty, describing clothing, accommodations, foods, local customs, transportation, a few notable personalities, and more.
      Includes bibliographical references and index.
      ISBN: 0–8225–3073–2 (lib. bdg. : alk. paper)
      1. China—Civilization—221 B.C.–960 A.D.—Juvenile literature. 2. China—Guidebooks—Juvenile literature. [1. China—Civilization, 221 B.C.–960 A.D. 2. China—Social life and customs—221 B.C.–960 A.D.] I. Title: Ancient China. II. Passport to history (Minneapolis, Minn.).
    DS748.13.S54 2004
    931—dc21   2003005619

Manufactured in the United States of America
1 2 3 4 5 6 – JR – 09 08 07 06 05 04

CONTENTS

INTRODUCTION

GETTING STARTED

Welcome to Passport to History. You will be traveling through time and space to ancient China in the first century B.C. In your travels you will find answers to questions such as:

➤ **What's going on in ancient China?**

➤ **Which local food should I try?**

➤ **Who will I meet while I'm there?**

➤ **Where should I stay?**

➤ **What do I wear?**

Remember that you are going back in time to a distant culture. Some of the things that you own didn't exist during this period. There were no cameras then. That's why the pictures in this book are either drawings or photographs made after the invention of photography. They didn't have electricity either. So forget about packing your video games, hair dryers, cameras, medicines, watches, cell phones, and the other modern conveniences that you think would make your stay more comfortable. Just read this guide, and you'll be able to do as the locals do—and they manage just fine, as you will see.

This relief carving of a Chinese emperor being pulled in a cart dates to the Han dynasty (206 B.C.–A.D. 220). Findings like this have helped historians figure out how people lived in China during that period of time.

NOTE TO THE TRAVELER

The ancient Chinese left literature, official documents, artwork, tools, and buildings that provide a window into their lives. Archaeologists study the remains of ancient Chinese structures and examine the remains of artifacts that have survived. Historians study texts left by the ancient writers, such as the famous Chinese historian Sima Qian (145–87? B.C.), whose works, known as the *Records of the*

Grand Historian, give a detailed history of China up to the Han dynasty of Emperor Wu Di, who ruled 141–87 B.C. A dynasty is when members of the same family rule over a period of time.

Archaeologists continue to uncover new clues to the culture of ancient China, sometimes making their finds by sheer good luck. In 1974 a great discovery was made when Chinese peasant farmers who were digging a well near a great burial mound came upon pieces of terracotta pottery in the earth. Archaeologists were called in. They found themselves excavating row after row of pottery soldiers and horses— a whole army of terra-cotta warriors that had been sent to guard the emperor in his tomb. Each warrior is amazingly lifelike, molded with his armor, and each statue is clearly a portrait of a different man. Only

In 1974 an army of terra-cotta warriors was found in the tomb of Emperor Qin Shi Huangdi.

about one tenth of the site has been excavated, and no one knows what new wonders may yet be found. But so far, archaeologists have gained new insights into the clothing, armor, weapons, and even horse gear of China of more than two thousand years ago.

As new discoveries are made, archaeologists and historians continue to improve their understanding of life in ancient China. Therefore, while this book is a good starting place for your voyage to ancient China, it is always possible that you will find something that is different from the descriptions in this book. Make a note of it for future researchers.

SIDE TRIP TRIVIA

The clay warriors (left) came from the tomb of Qin Shi Huangdi, the founder of the Qin dynasty. Qin is pronounced "Chin," and the dynasty gave its name to the country, China, too. Emperor Qin Shi Huangdi was terrified of dying and decided to live forever by searching for a potion that would grant him immortality. That didn't work, of course, but his tomb is an underground palace.

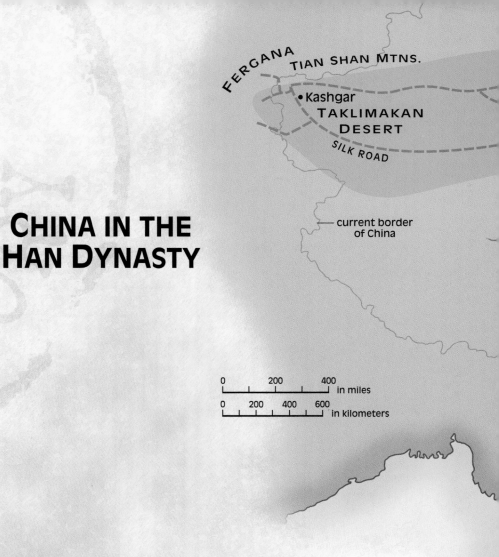

FERGANA TIAN SHAN MTNS.

•Kashgar TAKLIMAKAN DESERT

SILK ROAD

— current border of China

```
0         200       400
|----|----|----|----| in miles

0    200  400  600
|--|--|--|--|--|--| in kilometers
```

CHINA IN THE HAN DYNASTY

WHY VISIT ANCIENT CHINA?

China has an amazingly long history, one that stretches back thousands of years. That's too long for any traveler to visit everything within one lifetime! Instead, you can schedule a visit to just one era of China's past. And one certain time in ancient China, the time of the Han dynasty (206 B.C.–A.D. 220) is definitely worth the trip.

Check out the map. You'll see that Han China covers a large area of Asia, though it's not quite as big as modern China. The Chinese called their country the Middle Kingdom. They think it is the center of the universe. Maybe it isn't. But there's no denying Han China's influence on the world. So powerful was their legacy that to this day, the Chinese call themselves the Han. The list of inventions that come from the Han dynasty sounds almost too amazing to be true: paper, the wheelbarrow,

10

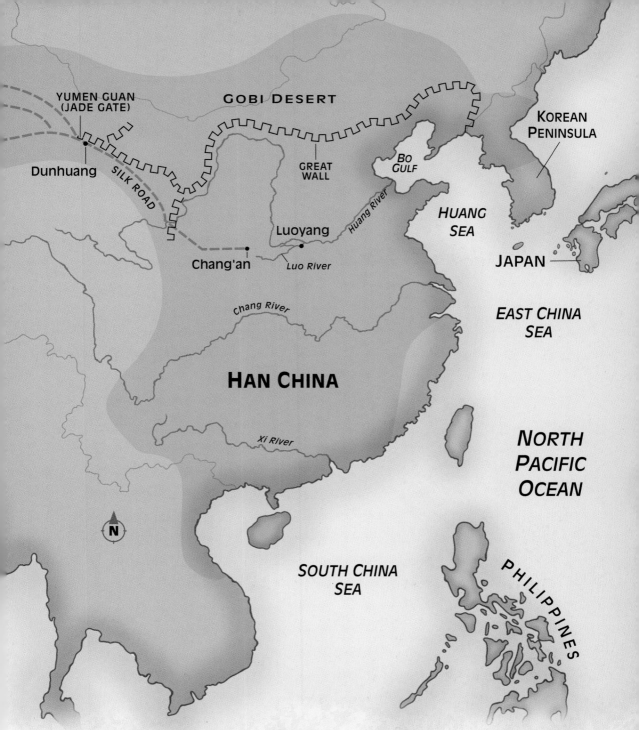

the compass, a form of seismograph to locate earthquakes, porcelain—
a type of fine ceramic—and much more. It was a great time for trade,
too. During the Han dynasty, the major trade route called the Silk Road
was established. It linked China with the rest of Asia and parts of Eu-
rope as far west as ancient Rome. The Han dynasty was a rich period
for the arts, too, including painting, pottery, weaving, and music.

THE BASICS

LOCATION LOWDOWN

Ancient China includes varied landscapes and climates, and it has some really spectacular scenery. To the east, China borders the Pacific Ocean. But don't plan to go swimming. The coastline's too rocky to have many safe beaches. And the water is pretty cold, too, at least for most of the way along the coast. After all, we're talking about a long coastline, one that runs in from present-day Korea the north all the way to modern Vietnam (where the water finally starts warming up). But even if you can't go swimming, there are some gorgeous views to be had of sparkling blue waves hitting the rocky cliffs.

To the west lie some fabulous mountain ranges, such as the snowcapped Tian Shan Mountains, which are both beautiful and awe inspiring. Also in the west are some truly awesome deserts, such as the terrible Taklimakan Desert with its fierce heat and lack of water. There is also the Gobi Desert, home to wandering nomads and the only truly wild horses in the world.

But there's also plenty of scenery in China for tourists who may have gentler tastes. If you travel south, you can find mile after mile of farmland. The green fields and rolling hills set among meandering rivers are soothing to the eye.

Handy WORDS & PHRASES

So dangerous is the Taklimakan Desert that it was given the name "Taklimakan," meaning (loosely translated), "You go in, you don't come out again."

Giant sand dunes of the Taklimakan Desert dwarf modern-day camels and their riders.

The snowcapped Tian Shan Mountains stretch across western China.

CLIMATE

You can find pretty much any type of weather you might want in ancient China. There are several different climate zones within its boundaries. The north gets cold enough for a good deal of snow in the winter, and those Tian Shan Mountains are snowcapped year-round. The desert lands to the west can be incredibly hot in the summer and shockingly cold in the winter.

Much of the land that lies in between these extremes is milder, with the usual four seasons. What clothing you take will depend not only on the local fashions but also on the type of weather you expect to encounter. Of course, no matter what climate you expect, you're not going to want to stand out by wearing modern sneakers or a name-brand jacket. You'll find plenty of choices in the WHAT TO WEAR section starting on page 49.

LOCAL TIME

You won't find wristwatches in ancient China. You won't find alarm clocks, either. That doesn't mean that people here aren't able to tell time. What you will find is that the local people tell time by the sun and by using water clocks.

Unfortunately, none of the Chinese water clocks, even the most intricate and complex of them, is completely accurate. So if you want to make a morning appointment with someone in ancient China, better make it for "about ten o'clock."

A water clock works by letting water drip at a regular rate through a small hole into a container marked with the numbers of hours. China didn't invent the water clock. Ancient Egyptians were using their own water clocks as far back as 1500 B.C. But the Chinese have developed some intricate mechanical water clocks, including some that not only tell time but also show the position of the sun, moon, and stars.

Incidentally, if you're thinking of asking someone to meet you over the weekend, forget that idea. The Chinese don't have weekends. Many people work every day, year-round, taking time off only for festivals. If you tell someone that you enjoy Saturday because you don't have to go to school or work that day, they may think you're making up a story— or else that you're an incredibly lazy person.

An early version of the Chinese calendar dates back to at least the fourteenth century B.C. Like our own, it divides the year into twelve months. But it's a lunar calendar, one that counts months from full moon to full moon. Because the moon's schedule varies a bit, the years on a Chinese calendar aren't always exactly the same length. A year might have as few as 353 days or as many as 355 days.

The first month of a new year varied from place to place in ancient China. Finally, Qin Shi Huangdi, emperor from 221 B.C. to 210 B.C., reformed the calendar calculation system, so that everyone across China was using

Qin Shi Huangdi was the first emperor of a unified China. Before him, China was made up of a number of warring states.

the same calendar. The calendar, still used in modern times, counts years in cycles of sixty years. These sixty-year cycles are broken down into twelve-year cycles. Each of these twelve years is named for an animal.

THE NAME GAME

At first you may have trouble figuring out how Chinese names work. You may think that you're being properly polite, and then learn that you have, instead, been rudely calling someone you've only just met by his or her first name.

In Western cultures such as in the United States, we put our personal names, such as James or Alice, first, and then add our family names, such as Smith or Williams. But in China, showing the family you belong to is more important than showing who you are as an individual. Knowing who your family is tells everyone where you fit into life. So the family name always comes first. If you're born into the Li family and were given the personal name of Yuen, your proper name is Li Yuen.

LANGUAGE LESSON

One of the things you're sure to notice, almost as soon as your trip begins, is that not everyone you meet in ancient China speaks the same way. We're not just talking about the problem of dealing with several accents. Because China is made up of several different nationalities joined together into one country, you may hear eight different languages in the marketplace—and yet learn that all of them are called Chinese.

Don't worry, as a tourist, you won't be expected to learn all of them. If you can manage the main language, which is called Mandarin Chinese, you're sure to find that almost everyone will understand you.

As China expands to include more and more people within its borders, things become even more complicated. There are about fifty non-Chinese languages also spoken in China. Don't worry about these, either. Unless you're planning to do a lot of traveling outside the cities, you won't really have to worry about Uighur, Kazakh, or any of those other languages.

HITTING THE BOOKS

Not everyone in ancient China can read or write. In fact, up until the reign of Emperor Wu Di, there weren't even any schools. But the emperor felt that education was the key to good government, so he started a system of public schools. Now you can find a school in every province, where some kids learn everything from reading and writing to philosophy, math, literature, and art.

Of course, the richest families wouldn't even think of sending their children to public schools. Instead, they hire private tutors to teach their children.

The main school in the public system, the Grand School, is in the capital city of Chang'an, which is known as Xi'an in modern times. When it opened, there were only fifty students registered. Since then, the enrollment has shot up to several thousand, with many more young

Education became available to more Chinese during the Han dynasty. In this illustration, scholars translate classical texts.

people being turned away because there isn't enough room for them. Maybe the emperor will order still more schools to be built.

One thing you'll notice is that only boys are admitted to the public schools. People believe that girls don't need to learn reading and writing to get married and be wives and mothers. Yet some women do manage to get decent educations, particularly if they have parents who are willing to teach them or hire tutors for them.

WRITING IS ART

Chinese writing doesn't look like English, wich uses Roman letters. Chinese characters aren't letters, but a form of writing in which each character stands for a word. The Chinese don't write with pens or pencils, either. The Chinese appreciate beautiful writing, called calligraphy. You'll probably notice someone writing with a brush. These brushes are usually made of hair, like paintbrushes. There are three types that most people prefer—white goat's hair, black rabbit's hair, and yellow weasel's hair. Depending on what type of writing or calligraphy you plan to do, you'd choose a brush that has hard, medium, or soft bristles. Ordinary writing brushes usually have bamboo or wood handles, but there are also some really expensive ones that have handles of porcelain, ivory, or jade.

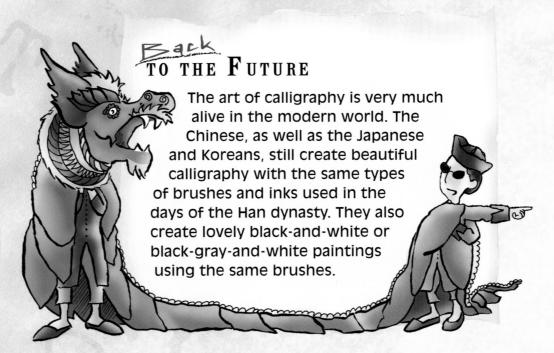

Back TO THE FUTURE

The art of calligraphy is very much alive in the modern world. The Chinese, as well as the Japanese and Koreans, still create beautiful calligraphy with the same types of brushes and inks used in the days of the Han dynasty. They also create lovely black-and-white or black-gray-and-white paintings using the same brushes.

The squid is part of a family of sea creatures known as cephalopods, which includes octopuses and cuttlefish. And yes, the squid (as well as many of its cephalopod cousins) can produce ink. When it's in danger, a squid ejects this ink as a dark cloud to confuse oncoming predators.

There are even some with mother-of-pearl inlaid designs worked into the wood.

A brush is useless without ink. Most ancient Chinese writers use an ink stick, which is a solid block of ink. Some people still use blocks of natural ink that's taken from a squid.

In the Han dynasty, though, you'll see more and more "artificial" ink sticks being used. These are made of a mixture of pine tar, oil, and lacquer. If you're planning to buy an ink stick, be sure to ask for the best and most popular brand: Yumi-mo. This brand is new in the Han dynasty.

But you can't write with a solid ink stick. You'll also need an inkstone, which is a stone with a small hollow carved into it. A little water in the hollow, a little grind of the ink stick against the stone, and you have liquid ink,

These calligraphy tools are from a later period than the Han, but the tools have changed little over the years.

ready for the brush. It's not easy to get exactly the right consistency, not too thick or too watery, but that comes with practice.

Now you'll need something to write on. You already know that paper

Chinese workers dip a mold into liquified paper pulp and hang the sheets to dry.

was invented during the Han dynasty, and there are many different types and brands of paper. You'll probably run into Fang-ma-tan, Ba-quao, Xuan-quan, Ma-quan-wan, Ju-yan, and Han-tan-po brands. All of these are perfectly good. Shop around in the marketplace till you find the type of paper that you like the best.

If you want to go the whole way, you can also get yourself a brush holder, an ink box to hold your ink stick, and a paperweight to hold your paper in place. You can find these writing accessories in every marketplace or in artists' stores. Depending on how much you want to spend, you can find writing accessories in every possible material from pure white porcelain to pricey carved jade to rare and costly coral.

WHICH CITIES TO VISIT

A wall surrounds Chang'an to keep out attacking northern tribes such as the Xiongnu (shown above battling a Chinese warrior).

CHANG'AN

This bustling capital of the Han dynasty is definitely the city that you should plan to see first. It is, after all, the second largest city in the ancient world. Only Rome, center of the Roman Empire, is bigger.

Founded by Liu Pang, who also founded the Han dynasty back in 206 B.C., Chang'an (present-day Xi'an) is clearly the result of careful city planning. If you look at a city map, you'll see that its streets and avenues are set out on a grid system, north, south, east, and west. This makes it difficult for a visitor to get lost, since all the streets are straight and numbered.

You can feel safe from any outside attacks in Chang'an. The city is surrounded by a strong outer wall. Soldiers man the wall's guard towers night and day. There is always the chance of an attack from the northern tribes.

While sightseeing in Chang'an, don't forget that since it's the center of Chinese government, there will be some restrictions placed on tourists. For instance, you might decide that you want to see the imperial palace. Don't be disappointed if all you get to see is the massive white outer wall. Security has to be tight for the head of any government. You probably won't get to see any of the lovely murals that are painted on the inner walls of the royal palace, either, but official visitors to the palace report that these murals show scenes of court life in bright and lively colors.

In addition, Chang'an is home to most of the main governmental buildings, such as the law court, which you will easily recognize because it looks as massive as a fortress. You probably will only be able to see the court and other government buildings from the outside too.

If you're lucky, you could get a glimpse of Chinese royal life through the gates of the royal palace (left) in Chang'an. This tomb sculpture represents a palace gate.

This model of a house was found in a Han dynasty tomb. This view shows the inside of the courtyard behind the garden wall.

You won't be able to see more than the outside walls of private houses either. Houses in Chang'an, as well as in some of the other cities, are built within a walled courtyard that encircles the house and garden. Those houses that don't have separate walls around them have a windowless wall of the house facing the street.

Famous residents of the city include the emperor, of course, though it's unlikely that you'll get a chance to see more than a glimpse of him. Emperor Wu Di is a very busy man right now. He is currently sending military expeditions into western China against the warlike nomads, the Xiongnu. He is also sending diplomatic missions to

Emperor Wu Di assumed control of the Han dynasty in 141 B.C. He increased security to protect China from the Xiongnu, northern nomadic tribes, by expanding sections of the Great Wall, which stretches across much of northern China.

Horses were prized possessions in Han China. This pair of bronze horse sculptures was found in China's Gansu province in eastern China.

Central Asia to find allies against this enemy. Wu Di's recent conquest of Fergana, a region far to the west, has enabled him to import some of the Heavenly Horses from there, a fine breed that will be valuable in the cavalry (mounted troops) and help the Chinese keep the Silk Road open.

The members of the royal council also live in Chang'an. Some of them have apartments within the palace walls, while others live in fine mansions near the palace grounds. These mansions are hidden behind high wood or brick walls.

The many workers necessary for the running of a government, from file

TAKE IT from a Local

Horses are the foundation of military might, the great resource of the state.

—*Ma Yuan, first century* B.C.

clerks to judges, also live in Chang'an. Their houses aren't so grand. They are often wooden or bamboo buildings crowded close together on narrow streets. Just as in every other large city, Chang'an has a poorer section of town, too. Here people live packed together in ramshackle houses with no toilets or running water.

Because it is the seat of government, Chang'an's streets are usually crowded with busy people hurrying to and from work. When you add to that confusion the crowds filling the city's marketplaces and the never-ending flow of carts, wagons, and foot travelers, you'll find that Chang'an is a bustling city.

Tourists do need to be a little careful. Prosperity doesn't mean that Chang'an doesn't have its problems. There are plenty of pickpockets. The city also has some trouble with roving street gangs. See the section on HOW TO STAY SAFE & HEALTHY starting on page 67 for warnings and advice.

LUOYANG

This ancient city is high on the list of places for a tourist to visit. It has some of the best archaeological sites and natural beauty in China. Luoyang, which is east of Chang'an, is older than the capital city—older, in fact, than all of the Han dynasty. No one is even sure just when Luoyang was founded or by whom. It gets its name because it lies on the north bank of the Luo River in the Yi-Luo River Basin.

Luoyang is a great place to visit if you want to see the ruins of the earlier Chinese dynasties. There are some here that date back to over two thousand years before the start of the Han dynasty. You can go to nearby Mangshan Mountain and walk among tombs from the Zhou dynasty before China was a unified country. Nearby are ruins of buildings from past ages, too, including some from the Shang dynasty that may date from about 1700 B.C. Most of these ruins, which consist mainly of the half-fallen walls of palaces and houses, are well within walking distance of the city center, and you can easily and safely visit them on foot. Although there are no formal tour guides, you may be able to hire someone to tell you about the ruins. Watch out! He or she may embroider the truth with some fantastic stories about dragons and fairies as well.

Luoyang is also a city for anyone who likes flowers, since it is noted for its fine gardens. It is a treat to walk by the river to enjoy the combination of green and flowery gardens and clear blue water.

Chinese dragons aren't the scary creatures of the fairy tales you have read. Most Chinese dragons, according to the stories, are wise and intelligent. Some of them are godlike beings in charge of the rain or major rivers. Chinese dragons will sometimes help humans, especially emperors. Imperial robes often feature a finely embroidered five-clawed imperial dragon.

Famous residents of Luoyang include the court historian and writer Sima Qian. Luoyang citizens also claim that their city is the home of the first seismograph. This machine, which detects earthquakes, is in the form of a bronze vessel with nine dragons facing out in a circle around it. Each dragon holds a bronze ball in its jaws. An earthquake will cause the ball to fall from the dragon that faces in the direction of the quake. Help then can be sent more quickly to that region.

According to modern-day research, it appears that the world's first earthquake detector (right)—invented by the Chinese—actually worked!

<u>Back</u> TO THE FUTURE

China has always experienced strong earthquakes. In 1976 extremely powerful quakes hit the city of Tangshan in eastern China and killed hundreds of thousands of people.

THE COUNTRYSIDE

If time allows, you should also plan to take a side trip outside the cities. That will give you a feel for the real China. Ancient China needs as much food as the farmers can grow to feed its people. That's why so much of the land that surrounds the cities is given over to farms.

In the north, most of those farms grow vegetables, barley, and wheat. In the south, you'll see rice farms. The rice paddies, or fields, are flooded for part of the growing season. They look like square or rectangular pools of water separated by narrow ridges of earth.

You're probably used to the sight of pigs and chickens, but keep an eye out for animals that may be more unusual to you. These include

This is a clay statue of a pig. Farmers raised pigs and other animals for food in ancient China.

Raised as work animals, rather than for meat, water buffalo provided the strength for pulling plows. An artist carved this small statue out of stone.

water buffalo and oxen, which farmers use to pull their plows and carts.

Try to visit a farmer at home. Farmhouses in ancient China are usually made of mud brick, with roofs made of reed thatching or, if the farmer can afford them, tiles.

You'll often find that the main floor of a Chinese farmhouse has deliberately been built a story or half a story below ground level. The surrounding earth creates a natural insulation that keeps everyone in the house cooler in the summer and warmer in the winter.

If you do decide to visit a farm in ancient China, don't expect any luxuries. You may not even get a bed, just a mattress filled with straw on

Carvings and figurines found in Han dynasty tombs often showed scenes from daily life. This relief carving shows a man driving an ox-drawn plow.

Tech Talk

To make a mud brick, you first need four pieces of wood nailed into a rectangle. Mix up some mud and add straw to it for extra strength. Fill the rectangle, scrape off any extra mud, and let it dry in the sun. Remove the wooden frame, and you have a mud brick ready for use.

the floor. There won't be any indoor plumbing, either. You'll have to head around back for the outhouse. Because the houses have no running water, the women of the house have to carry water in buckets from the village well or the river. It's hard work for them, so be careful not to waste a drop.

Don't expect any late nights. Ancient Chinese farmers get up early and go to bed early.

A Chinese farm has its barns and other buildings near or around the farmhouse. If you happen to notice one that's tall and narrow, that's a granary. It's where farmers stores their harvested grain.

MONEY MATTERS

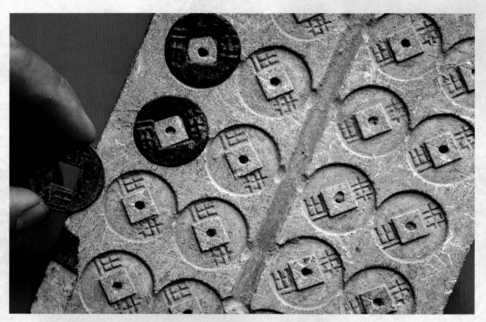

Half-liang coins have holes in their centers so they can be strung on a cord.

The Han dynasty Chinese have a standardized system of coins. The most common is called a half-liang. Made of copper, a half-liang has a square hole in the middle. Forget about carrying a wallet. People string half-liangs on rope or cord so that they don't lose their change. It's an easy and convenient way to carry your money—unless you're carrying around too much cash! Then it will feel pretty heavy by the end of a sightseeing day.

There's talk about a new coin that is soon going to be issued by Queen Lu, the emperor's wife. It will be called the zhu. It will look like the half-liang but be lighter, so that people will be able to carry more coins more easily.

POSTCARDS FROM CHINA

You won't be able to send a postcard to the folks back at home in the twenty-first century. But you might be surprised to learn that you will be able to send a letter to someone anywhere in ancient China. The Chinese have a pretty swift and accurate way of delivering mail by a network of couriers on horseback. Inns are set at regular intervals along all the main roads to give the mail carriers places to rest. These inns also act as local post offices. A courier might ride to one of the inns from the east, drop off mail that's to be picked up by a southbound courier, change horses, and ride on with mail that's to be delivered to the west.

Handy
WORDS & PHRASES

The half-liang's shape has given it a nickname, Square Hole Brother.

The fastest delivery is saved for the most urgent mail, such as military dispatches. But there are also several classes of regular mail, too, from first class down to the ancient Chinese version of bulk mail. The slowest class of mail is delivered by a courier who simply walks from village to village, dropping the letters off along the way. Mail can also be labeled "express." If you send an express letter, you get a guarantee that it will arrive on time and unopened.

To send a letter, you roll up the letter scroll yourself, tie it with cord so it can't come open, then seal it with wax and make sure that the wooden tag with the name and address of the person receiving the mail is firmly attached. There aren't any envelopes. When you hand over the letter to the courier, he stamps it with the time and date, and off it goes on its way.

An illustrated manuscript from the 1600s shows Emperor Wu Di receiving a letter sent through his efficient mail system.

How to Get Around

By Water

You may be surprised to see canals in China linking the many rivers. There's a good reason for this. Roads aren't paved, and a good rainstorm quickly turns them to mud. In dry weather, they're dust. A wagon may break down or lose a wheel. A horse can go lame. The rivers and canals change all that. These watery highways link together the cities and trading centers. People can get around quickly and easily by boat, and food and merchandise can be transported without any worries about muddy roads or broken wagon wheels. In fact, people have started living on their boats. You may see everyone from a grandma down to the smallest baby on board.

Hot Hint

Children living on boats quickly learn to swim, and babies wear life preservers made of hollow bamboo.

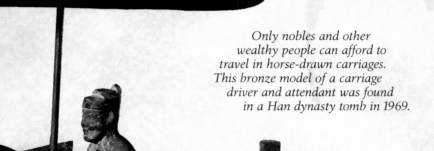

*Only nobles and other
wealthy people can afford to
travel in horse-drawn carriages.
This bronze model of a carriage
driver and attendant was found
in a Han dynasty tomb in 1969.*

BY LAND

If you want to see parts of China that aren't
on the rivers or canals, you're probably going
to have to go over land. This won't be very easy
for you because there isn't any regularly sched-
uled transport. You can walk, of course, though that's
a slow and dusty way to travel. The main roads, which the
express mail couriers use, aren't too bad, since they're broad and lined
with shade trees. But side roads are going to be narrow, unpaved, and full
of potholes. They also won't be as safe, because once you get out of the
tourist areas, there well may be bandits lurking about. And the farther
away from cities you get, out past farm country, the more likely you are
to run into nomad raiders.

You might think about renting a horse. Han China does have horses,
but they are expensive to own. Only rich people or the noble class uses
them, traveling in carriages pulled by one or two horses and shaded by
umbrellas. The carriages look elegant, but they don't have any springs.
Riding in one means a lot of bouncing and jouncing, so a trip of any
length is pretty rough on the spine.

• Kashgar
TAKLIMAKAN
DESERT

current border ——
of China

Although everyone uses the term *Silk Road*, which was coined in the nineteenth century, there actually are several different roads to the west during the Han dynasty (see map pages 10–11). They all go over the same ground as far as the town of Dunhuang on the edge of the Taklimakan Desert. From there, the northern route leads through the Yumen Guan, or Jade Gate, then edges the Gobi Desert and follows the line of the Tian Shan Mountains away from the Taklimakan, down to the town of Kashgar.

The other route skirts the southern edges of the Taklimakan Desert, finally turning north again to join up with the alternative route at Kashgar. Other routes branch off from the southern road, heading on down to the shores of the Caspian Sea. But Silk Road has stuck as the name for them all.

MAJOR WATERWAYS OF THE HAN DYNASTY

You might be able to catch a lift from a peasant with an ox-drawn cart. That's not going to be a comfortable way to travel, either. It will be bumpy, dusty, and slow.

If you still feel adventurous, you might want to join up with one of the caravans (a company of travelers on pack animals) heading out over the Silk Road to the west. It's safer traveling with a group than traveling alone.

In addition to silk, caravans to and from ancient China carry a whole catalog of precious things:

• Gold and silver
• Ivory
• Precious stones
• Ceramics
• Jade
• Lacquerware
• Bronze
• Plants and animals

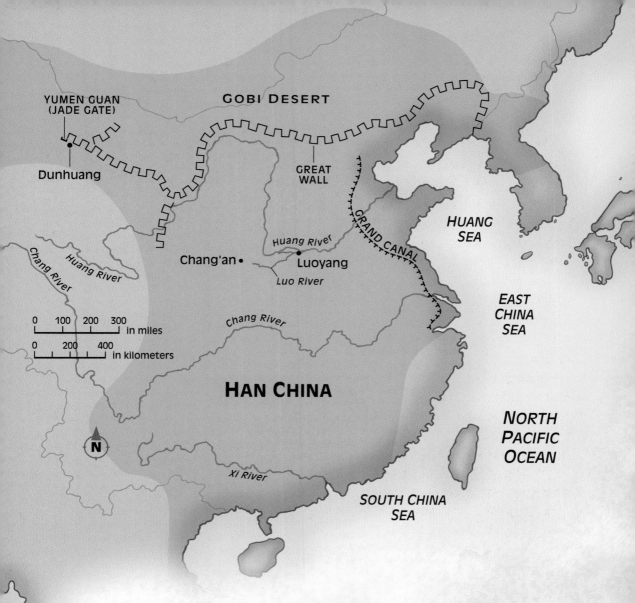

YUMEN GUAN
(JADE GATE)

GOBI DESERT

Dunhuang

GREAT
WALL

GRAND CANAL

HUANG
SEA

Chang River

Huang River

Huang River

Chang'an •

Luoyang

Luo River

EAST
CHINA
SEA

Chang River

0   100   200   300
in miles

0   200   400
in kilometers

HAN CHINA

N

NORTH
PACIFIC
OCEAN

Xi River

SOUTH CHINA
SEA

Not everything originally packed in ancient China travels the whole length of the Silk Road. If you do go with a caravan, you'll probably see some goods bartered for others along the way. Objects sometimes change hands from caravan to caravan without ever getting to the end of the road.

Traveling the Silk Road is exciting, but crossing the desert and mountains isn't for anyone who hasn't been working out. And unless you have a year or more to spare, you'd better not try such a long journey.

36

LOCAL CUSTOMS
& MANNERS

WHAT YOU CAN
EXPECT FROM THE LOCALS

You'll find that the Chinese will be polite but a little standoffish at first, at least until they know who you are. People in ancient China are very conscious of everyone's proper place in life. Once you get to know people though, you'll find that they are just as warm and friendly as anyone else.

SOCIAL STANDING

At the top of the social ladder is, of course, the emperor, with the nobility just below. After that, everyone is divided into four major classes. First come the scholars, since they can read and write. Next come the peasants. Surprised? The peasants, after all, provide the food that keeps everyone alive. Next come the artists and craftspeople, because their skills make everything people need, from weapons to weavings. The lowest class is made up of the merchants. Merchants have such a low ranking because they don't produce anything. They simply sell things.

Peasant farmers, like this one caring for a pig in its sty, are valued in Chinese society because they produce food. This model is made of glazed terra-cotta.

WOMEN

Ancient China isn't the best or the worst time to be a woman. The man of the house is usually expected to be the boss of the family, but the Han dynasty woman isn't assumed to be a second-class citizen, either. She's supposed to be modest and not boast—but that's true of every member of this polite society. There are no actual laws forbidding a woman from learning, but it is almost impossible for a woman to be successful except by marrying a successful man.

SLAVERY

There are slaves in ancient China, although it's not a subject people talk about very much. Some slaves were war captives. Some were sold into slavery because they couldn't pay off their debts. Still others were born slaves. In the old days, before Emperor Wu Di came to the throne, slaves had no rights and were often abused, injured, or killed by their owners. Now slaves have been granted some rights. There are even laws to protect them. You can read more about this in the LAW AND ORDER section on page 68.

One chore of servants and slaves is to light oil lamps. This bronze oil lamp has been sculpted in the shape of a servant holding an oil lamp.

A Problem with Merchants

Even though they are low in status, some of the merchants have upset the Chinese class system by becoming rich. In fact, some have become so wealthy that they have bought themselves carriages and mansions, just like the nobles. This is making both the nobles and the peasants angry. Both groups have been petitioning the emperor to pass a law to forbid merchants from showing off like this. But so far, the merchants are free to do as they wish with their money.

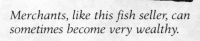

Merchants, like this fish seller, can sometimes become very wealthy.

Local Manners

China is a land of politeness and custom. You'll have to be careful what you say and do so that you don't accidentally insult someone.

People bow to each other when they meet. The person with the lower status makes the deeper bow. It's polite for a younger person to bow more deeply to an older one. You'll soon realize that in ancient China, older people are respected for their wisdom. Children are taught that it's proper to honor and obey their elders, and they grow up expecting to care for their parents in their old age.

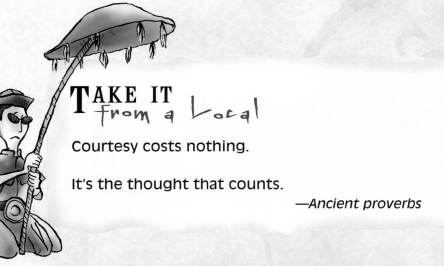

Take It from a Local

Courtesy costs nothing.

It's the thought that counts.

—*Ancient proverbs*

After you've been properly introduced, it's time to start a conversation. It's usually safe to begin with simple things, like the weather, and wait for the older person to start any other subjects. Don't ask any personal questions, particularly not to women. It just isn't polite.

What if you're invited to someone's house? It's considered polite to bring a gift, something simple, like candy or flowers. But you'd better learn some more customs before you go.

Giving two gifts is a good idea, because there's a Chinese saying that blessings go in pairs. But never give any gifts in public. That, too, is thought to be immodest and rude. And never give four of anything, because the written Chinese word for four looks like the Chinese word for death. That's not exactly a nice present!

If you're going to understand the ancient Chinese people, you'll have to learn that for the Chinese it's not the person but the family that's important. Keeping the family's honor is thought far more important than worrying about personal goals.

The Chinese admire modesty. If someone compliments you on the way you speak Chinese, don't say, "Thank you." Instead, say, "My Chinese is very poor." You'll also never hear Chinese parents showing off about their children. No matter how proud they may be of the youngsters, they'll sound unhappy about them in public so that they don't seem to be bragging.

LOCAL BELIEFS

The ancient Chinese have two different systems of belief. The first is named Confucianism, and the second is called Taoism.

Confucianism is the official state belief. It gets its name from a wandering scholar of the fifth century B.C., Confucius, also called Kong Fuzi, which means "Master Kong." Confucianism prizes education and

opposes war as harmful to the state. It proposes that most of society's problems come from people forgetting their proper stations in life and rulers losing their virtue. It promotes proper conduct and social harmony rather than our Western ideals of liberty and equality. Confucianism names five major relationships: between the ruler and the subject, between husband and wife, between parents and children, between older and younger brothers, and between friends.

Taoism is the second belief system in Han China. It started out in the sixth century B.C. as a form of philosophy. Basically, Taoism states that there is an eternal Tao, which is a vital but mysterious force that unifies everything in the universe. Taoists avoid wealth, power, or anything else that they think would distract them from the Tao.

The Tao religion is based on a folk religion that made gods of real people who showed unusual powers when they lived. The Tao priests send the

prayers of the people to these gods or to the greater divinities (godlike beings) that represent aspects of the Tao way.

In the Taoist religion, Lord Xuan Wu, the Dark Lord of the North, is a widely worshipped deity (god). He can control the elements and wield mighty magic. Some of the other major deities of the Taoist heaven include the Jade Emperor, who rules that heaven, and Wen Chang, the god of culture and the patron of scholars, students, and bureaucrats.

You may also hear some even older Chinese myths that explain how the world came into being or how all creation is divided into yin and yang. Yin is the darker half, the earth, and everything female, while yang is the lighter half, the sky, and everything male. There can be no perfect happiness or perfect health unless yin and yang are in equal balance.

Chinese men and boys unroll a scroll bearing the circular yin and yang symbol signifying balance in life.

Hot Hint

If you get out into the countryside, look for the village shrines. Each village has at least one shrine dedicated to the earth god. He's the god of the common people, who often refer to him as Grandpa to show how they believe he takes care of them.

People in China may follow the state belief of Confucianism. But they may also follow ancient folk beliefs and paint a tiger on a house wall to keep away danger or wear a charm in the shape of a dragon for protection against evil.

HOLIDAYS

If you happen to be in ancient China sometime between late January and late February, you'll have a chance to experience the most important Chinese holiday, the New Year. But unless you are part of a Chinese family, you won't see the whole days-long celebration.

To prepare for a new year, everyone first thoroughly cleans house and puts on new clothing. People make sure they settle all their debts. There aren't any wild New Year's Eve parties. Instead, New Year's Eve and New Year's Day, as well as the first day after that, are spent with family and close friends, praying and exchanging small gifts of money wrapped in red for good luck. The third day of the New Year is called Quarrel Day. If you quarrel on this day, you're supposed to have a lot of arguments all through the year.

It's not till the fifteenth day after the New Year that there are public celebrations. You'll find brightly colored lanterns hanging everywhere, marked with symbols for happiness, health, and good luck.

Another holiday you may experience is the Ching Ming Festival. It takes place in spring, usually in April. This is a day for the Chinese to honor their ancestors. You'll see many people at cemeteries and find willow branches hung in every doorway. It's believed that the willow wards off evil spirits.

PREDICTING THE FUTURE

The ancient Chinese are fascinated with learning about the future. You may get to watch a seer, or prophet, using oracle bones in a marketplace. Someone will ask a question such as, "Will my caravan be attacked by bandits?" The seer, the person doing the predicting, will then put a few bones into a fire. When the bones crack from the heat, the seer will pull them out and interpret the cracks to answer the question.

You may also get to see a form of predicting the future that makes use of stalks of the yarrow, a tall plant with a large yellow flower head. There's a belief that says the yarrow is magically wise: the longer and older the stalks, the wiser the plant. Someone telling the future with yarrow stalks tosses them on the ground, then reads the pattern they form.

There are also forms of prediction that you're not likely to see unless you enlist in the Chinese army—which is not recommended for the casual tourist. Before Emperor Wu Di's generals make any crucial moves, they consult their seers. The seers in turn depend on signs from the heavens. Sometimes they read messages in the winds. To do this correctly, a seer must use a compass, since the wind's message depends on the direction from which it's blowing.

Cloud formations, it's believed, may also carry a message. At night the positions of stars and planets may deliver messages to the seers. The most alarming messages seem to come from the most exciting events: comets and eclipses of the sun or moon.

Ancient Chinese prophets use compasses for divination (the practice of seeking to foretell the future) long before sailors use them for navigation. In the Han dynasty, navigational compasses are made of lodestone or magnetite ore. Chinese scientists of the era understand that these ores will point naturally toward the magnetic north pole. For the practice of divination, the spoon-shaped compasses are placed on cast bronze plates called heaven-plates. The plates are engraved with astrological symbols (symbols based on the position of the sun, stars, moon, and planets) as well as with geographical directions (north, south, east, west).

BIRTHDAY GREETINGS

When a Chinese baby is one month old, his or her relatives send the news to their local earth god through special offerings. Everyone breathes a sigh of relief when the baby reaches one year old, because that usually means he or she has decided to live.

After that, although a family may celebrate birthdays every year, the important birthdays come with longer spaces in between. One of these is the fifty-first birthday. To celebrate it, children give their parent a wooden screen that's decorated with symbols of long life. The sixty-first birthday is celebrated with a gift that may seem odd: a coffin. But this is the family's way of assuring that the person will someday have an honorable burial. A man who lives until seventy-one is awarded with a special robe and given a walking cane with a jade

Families in ancient China celebrate a sixty-fifth birthday with a handsome gift coffin.

45

handle carved in the shape of a bird. If the man lives until eighty-one, the emperor himself is notified of the birthday and has a memorial arch raised in his honor. And if he lives until ninety-one, he is honored with government greetings four times a year.

A woman doesn't get official government greetings, but she still may have her birthday honored. For instance, if a woman makes it into her seventies or older, her family might give her a pretty silver hairpin worked into the sign *shou,* meaning "longevity."

MARRIAGE VOWS

You may or may not get to see a wedding procession while you're visiting China. It may surprise you to learn that the bride and groom don't get to choose each other as mates. Instead parents negotiate the joining of their families with the help of a matchmaker. It's all very formal, including matching up the birth dates and horoscopes of the two young people and sending letters of proposal and acceptance. It's the custom for parents to give their daughter valuable presents as her dowry, which becomes part of the new couple's wealth. Although much of the dowry goes to the husband, many young brides are given jewelry or hairpins which they can wear to show off their family's wealth.

You won't see a white wedding dress at a Chinese wedding. On the day of the wedding, the bride rides to the home of her groom in a red sedan chair covered with a red veil. This wedding procession may also include lantern bearers, banner carriers, people striking gongs, the matchmaker, and the attendants. The rest of the ceremony is private, strictly for the families involved.

Hot Hint

Red is the color of happiness in China. White is the Chinese color of death.

DEATH AND BEYOND

The ancient Chinese don't believe that death is the end of everything. They have a firm belief that their ancestors' souls continue to play an important role in their lives. People honor their ancestors so that the ancestors will in turn help them, the living. The emperor has an even more important family, since his ancestors are supposed to link him directly to the force of the universe itself. He may spend several hours a day in rituals to keep in touch with those ancestors.

When someone dies, the corpse is placed in its coffin. It remains at home, sometimes as long as forty-nine days. A white mourning sash is fastened over the front door of the house, and lanterns are placed on either side of it as a sign to others that a death has occurred.

The family dresses in robes of sackcloth, a rough fabric like burlap, and the men of the family add white sashes and head cloths. They sit on the floor beside the coffin until it is time for the procession to the burial site. The eldest son or closest male relative walks ahead of the coffin, and the rest of the family follow it. Depending on the family's wishes and wealth, the procession may include men carrying lanterns with the family's name, musicians, and even professional mourners.

Ordinary people are content with ordinary graves, or maybe a family tomb. But emperors are different. The Han emperors and the Qin dynasty rulers before them make sure that their royal tombs are filled with all the rich things of their daily lives. In the older days, servants and guards were sacrificed so that they could accompany their royal master to the afterlife. Now, though, the emperors are content with ceramic warriors (right) to guard them. Some of the royal tombs are as fine as any palaces, complete with brightly painted murals on the walls. Most people today believe that you can't take it with you. The Chinese emperors believe that they can!

What to Wear

Clothes

You'll see Chinese people wearing two basic styles of clothing. The first is a two-piece suit made up of a tunic, or coat, and trousers. This style dates back a few hundred years, but the Han Chinese give it a more modern look by using colorful silks and bright embroidery in abstract patterns. The second style is a long robe of colorful, embroidered silk. In either style, people prefer wide sleeves and a loose fit. Some add sashes of contrasting colors to their outfits. In the winter, everyone who can afford them wears warm fur robes and heavy leather shoes.

But don't expect to be allowed to buy just any clothing. How you dress, from the type of fabric to the color of your robe, is a sign of your status. For instance, the higher you rank, the finer the silk you're allowed to wear. Darker colors are saved for ceremonial or official wear. Lighter colors are for everyday use. Just remember that you must never wear yellow or white. Yellow is the royal color, reserved for the emperor, and white is the Chinese color of mourning.

A farm family, of course, has no use for sheer silks. Husband and wife wear practical long tunics or tunics with loosely fitting pants usually woven of tough, undyed hemp. Hemp comes from the hemp plant, which is grown for its fibers.

Silk

Silk is the most important fabric in all China. It's soft and strong. It can be dyed in almost any color. And it can be embroidered and painted. Silk is worn throughout the empire. It's even exported along the Silk Road to Rome, where nobles complain that their wives' love of silk is bankrupting them.

Many Chinese, both men and women, wear long, colorfully embroidered robes with wide sleeves, as shown in this sculpture at left.

If you make friends with any of the merchants selling silk, you may hear the story behind the wonder fabric. Silk is made from the woven strands of the silkworm's cocoon. After it hatches from its egg, a silkworm is raised on a diet of mulberry leaves. After four or five weeks of steady eating, it spins its cocoon. But before it can escape as an adult moth, Chinese silk workers rinse the cocoon in hot water to kill the moth inside. This is tough luck for the moth, but provides the fibers that are then woven into silk.

The manufacture of silk is such a closely guarded secret that no one outside of China knows how it's done. The learned Roman scientist Pliny the Elder speculates in one of the books of his Natural History that "Silk is obtained by removing the down from the leaves" of a tree.

HAIR

You're sure to notice that Chinese men almost always wear hats, at least when they're out on the street. The most fashionable of these hats is made out of beautiful silk artfully folded into what look like ears.

Because the men wear hats, you won't have many chances to see their hairstyles. But this also means that if you're male, you won't have to worry too much about your hair.

Women, however, don't usually cover their heads. They keep their hair long and wear it arranged on top of their heads in all sorts of elaborate knots and buns. The styles are held in place by beautiful hairpins.

Outdoors, men wear hats of folded silk, as shown in this sculpture.

BEAUTY

City people in ancient China like to look their best. The women wear makeup that is often made with powdered pearl. This gives their skin a smooth, pale glow that is considered elegant. They also have their eyebrows carefully shaped, using tweezers just the way some modern women do.

Both men and women are fond of jewelry. What type of jewelry and how much of it you can wear depends on your standing in Chinese society. Poor people aren't likely to be wearing any jewelry other than a clay bead or two. But wealthier Chinese men and women wear a dazzling number of gold and jeweled necklaces and armbands. The women also wear delicate earrings and pearl headdresses. People can check how they look in highly polished bronze mirrors.

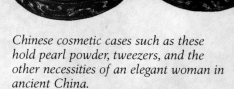

Chinese cosmetic cases such as these hold pearl powder, tweezers, and the other necessities of an elegant woman in ancient China.

51

What to See & Do

The Great Wall

The Great Wall is one of the ancient world's most incredible human-made marvels, one long line of walls and fortifications that runs uphill and down, about 1,500 miles across northern China. It's wide enough for three wagons to be driven abreast, and it's topped by great watchtowers at regular intervals.

The Great Wall was first built in the third century B.C., during the Qin dynasty, the one just before the Han dynasty began. The emperor Qin Shi Huangdi is supposed to have used more than 300,000 workers to build it, and many of them died during the construction. Emperor Wu Di has rebuilt parts of the wall that were in need of repair, and he extended it farther to the west to protect the Silk Road.

The purpose of the Great Wall is to keep out the wild nomadic tribes, the Mongols and Xiongnu, to China's north. So far it seems to be doing its job.

The Great Wall of China was begun by Qin Shi Huangdi. Emperor Wu Di later repaired parts of the Great Wall that had fallen into ruin. This photo shows what is left of the part of the Great Wall that was built during the Han dynasty.

This clay sculpture shows a troop of acrobats performing in the city marketplace.

FREE SHOWS

Try the marketplace in any city for free entertainment. On any day of the week, you are sure to find a variety of street musicians playing their instruments. There will be all sorts of performing jugglers and acrobats, too. You'll probably also find storytellers. Like any other street performers, these people live off what they earn from their audience, so don't forget to add some coins when they pass the hat.

OTHER THINGS TO SEE AND DO

At any time in any of the cities, there is likely to be some type of theater in the form of plays, concerts, or dance. You'll find few props in a theater production, but the bright costumes will make up for that lack. There may be music performances by full orchestras, though the instruments they play might sound strange to you. The instruments might include the pipa, which is

Clay sculpture of a dancer

Handy WORDS & PHRASES

The *erhu* is a kind of vertical Chinese fiddle. The *di* is a type of Chinese flute.

54

TAKE IT from a Local

Confucius said in his teachings that music to feed the soul is like food to feed the body.

a stringed instrument like a large zither or lute, bamboo flutes, and tuned series of chimes and bells. The emperor takes music of all sorts seriously. Emperor Wu Di's government even includes a Bureau of Music to collect old songs and organize new ones.

If you're in a city and in the mood for learning, you may enjoy taking a course in Chinese calligraphy or poetry composition. Don't expect to become an expert in either art form in only a lesson or two. It can take a lifetime for a calligraphy artist or a poet to master his or her art.

WHERE TO FIND SPORTS AND RECREATIONS

Ancient China has something for almost every sports fan. No, you won't find our modern sports of baseball, football, and basketball. But you will find just about everything else.

Interested in watching wrestling? Look for a *jaidoi* competition. That's a form of Chinese wrestling that goes back to about the third century B.C. The wrestlers wear ox horns on their heads and pretend to be two oxen fighting. Ask your local innkeeper for times and locations.

Whenever the weather is warm enough, you'll be able to find boating races. They take place on just about every major river in ancient China.

Gymnastics is popular in ancient China, and regular competitions for gymnasts are held year-round in many locations. You can also find archery competitions taking place from spring to fall. The wealthier people sometimes stage horse races, too.

Like to collect sports souvenirs? You can find them in ancient China. Go to any of these events or to stands in the marketplaces and you'll be able to find souvenirs in the shape of pottery figurines and sports-related paintings.

Go Fly a Kite

The Chinese love to fly kites. They believe that kites can carry prayers up into the heavens, but they also believe that kite flying is fun. You can buy yourself a colorful kite and join them. The first kites were made out of bamboo and silk, but the Chinese of the Han dynasty know how to make paper, so the kites they build are lighter and can be made in much more complex shapes. You may see kites made of sections of paper and bamboo that form tigers and even dragons.

The Chinese sometimes have kite-fighting contests. The contestants harden their kite strings with glue and add tiny bits of sharp stones. Each fighter tries to cut the strings of the other players' kites. The last kite in the air is the winner. Kite fighting takes skill and practice.

Emperor Wu Di has used kites in the shape of horrible monsters to frighten enemy armies. But you can fly kites just for fun along with the ancient Chinese people on any windy day.

Board Games

If you like playing board games *(left)*, you're going to like ancient China. On any sunny day, you'll find people playing board games similar to chess in the market-places and someone willing to play a game with you. But be careful! Many Chinese like to bet on games, and you can easily wind up losing a lot of money.

WHERE TO STAY

Emperor Qin Shi Huangdi traveled from town to town in an ornate carriage carried by servants, as shown in this watercolor on silk produced in the 1600s.

TIRED TRAVELERS

A large city such as Chang'an has plenty of inns for tired travelers. You'll be able to find a place to rest your sightseeing-weary head without too much trouble. Of course, just as in any other city, the quality of the place you find will depend on how much you can afford to pay. The better the inn, the closer it stands to the royal palace and the higher its prices. The sheets at the more expensive inns may well be made of silk. But don't

SIDE TRIP TRIVIA While good inns and the houses of the rich have private indoor toilets, the poor are stuck with using shared latrines and public drains.

expect a downy pillow at even the fanciest places, especially in the summer. Instead, you may find yourself trying to get comfortable on a porcelain headrest. If you like firm pillows, you'll really enjoy this! Even if you don't, you'll have to admit that it does keep your hair neat, and it allows the cool breezes to reach your neck.

Before you sleep, you'll want to wash off all that dust of travel. You can get a private bath in a good inn, with herbal-scented soap, too. There's no hot-and-cold running water, though. Instead, someone is going to have to lug the hot water to your tub, then empty the tub when you're finished. You'll have to pay extra for that service.

If you insist on a private bath, you're going to miss out on a typically Chinese experience. Many people prefer to go to the public baths. Going to the baths gives everyone the chance to catch up on gossip as they get clean. Give it a try. It's a nice way to meet people. Understand though that if you're really, really grungy, it's polite to take a private bath first! You'll find sellers of hot water for your tub in almost every major street.

For more personal matters, though, you won't have to leave the inn. The Chinese do have indoor toilets and a form of toilet paper!

PRIVATE HOMES

You aren't too likely to find lodging in someone's home unless you have become a friend of the family. But if you do receive an invitation, you'll find the Chinese home to be a charming place. Most homes, even the most elegant of manors, have the same basic shape. There is an outer wall with a gate on the south side, because that's said to be the direction of holiness. The house surrounds a central courtyard. Behind it is the family's garden. The richer the family, the more elaborate the garden.

The average house has a foundation of solid earth. On top of this is a base of stone slabs topped with wood columns or bamboo poles that form the walls. The slanted roof is made of terra-cotta tiles if you're in the city, thatch if you're in the country. You may see a good many roofs with upward curved ends. These are to prevent evil spirits from perching.

Many tile roofs in ancient China are decorated with terra-cotta figures of dragons and other beasts.

Some of the richer people decorate their roofs with terra-cotta figurines, such as dragons or other magical beasts, perched on the upturned ends.

The outer walls of the family compound are often made of brick, but the Chinese prefer wood for their houses. Remember that China experiences many earthquakes. Wooden buildings are less likely to hurt anyone if they collapse during a quake.

IMPORTANT
Safety Tip

In case of a quake, the worst thing that you can do is to rush blindly out into the street. All those terra-cotta tiles might be flying off their roofs and could hit you. Instead, if there's a quake, find a good, sturdy piece of furniture to stay under or a strong inner wall to lean against, and just wait till the authorities tell everyone what to do next. This is good advice in ancient China, but it's also good in the modern world.

What to Eat

Rice, a staple of the southern Chinese diet, is cooked in the big pot on this portable stove.

After all your sightseeing and shopping, you're bound to get hungry. Don't worry. You won't have any trouble finding a place to eat, from a full-sized restaurant to a little street stand. And you'll quickly learn that ancient Chinese food is every bit as varied as a Chinese dinner in modern times. Wheat, sheep, and goats from western Asia probably arrived in China long ago. Many new vegetables and fruits, such as pomegranates and grapes, are coming into China with the merchants traveling along the Silk Road.

About the only foods you won't find in ancient China are those that come from the New World (North and South America), like potatoes, tomatoes, chocolate, and pineapples. But with all the other food available, you won't miss them.

FOODS TO TRY

- Szechuan chicken
- Fried noodles
- Pork and rice

In the cities, you're likely to find pork and lamb, chicken, duck, and goose being served. You'll also find more unusual foods such as snake or dog. Don't worry, if you are served a dish containing dog meat—you won't be eating anyone's pet. There is a special type of hairless dog that's bred just for meat. Chinese cooking isn't heavy on meat, anyhow, but is a perfect blend of starch (rice in the south, wheat in the north), meat, and vegetable. From familiar dishes like stir-fried pork to the more un-usual, like coins of hairlike seaweed and chicken paste, you'll never have any trouble finding something interesting to eat.

If you're out in the country, of course, expect a simpler menu. Farm-ers can't afford to eat the elegant meals that are found in cities. Instead, if you stop at a country inn or are a guest at a farm, you'll find meals that are made up mostly of rice (in the south) or grain (in the north), plus vegetables and a bit of chicken or maybe a piece of fish. These coun-try meals are basic, but filling and delicious.

The Chinese usually cook their food by a method called stir-fry-ing. They invented this method because it's a great way to keep food flavors sealed in, but mostly because it's a great way to cook a meal using a minimum of fuel. Charcoal and coal, which are the main

Hot Hint

While wealthy Chinese have separate kitchens in their homes, poor people often don't have a kitchen at all. You will probably see them at the side of a road or a city street, cooking in the open air, using whatever scraps of wood or other fuel they can find.

FOODS TO TRY, at your own risk

- ► Bird's nest soup
- ► Roast dog
- ► Coins of hairlike seaweed and chicken paste
- ► Snake stir-fry

sources of fuel in ancient China, are expensive. When you are stir-frying, you first chop your food into small pieces, and then cook the pieces quickly in oil in a hot wok, a kind of high-sided pan, stirring constantly.

STICKING WITH CHOPSTICKS

Wherever you're eating, don't expect knives and forks. Those aren't found in China. Instead, the Chinese use *fai jee*, which we call chopsticks. If you plan to eat while in China, you'll need to learn to use them, too. Don't worry, it isn't a difficult skill to learn. And no one in ancient China will be rude enough to laugh at you if you make a mistake. You begin with one chopstick. Place it between your thumb and forefinger, resting it on the top joint of your middle finger. Then place the second chopstick above the first, and hold it like a pencil. The first chopstick doesn't move. But you can move the second chopstick freely up and down. Practice picking up something this way, and pretty soon you'll have the knack. A skillful chopstick user can pick up a single grain of rice.

Handy WORDS & PHRASES

Fai jee means "quick little boys," and if you watch someone eat who is used to eating with chopsticks, you'll understand the name. A skillful user can make the chopsticks seem to dart from bowl to mouth.

62

There are a few rules of good manners to remember about using chopsticks. Never play with them or point at anyone with them. That's considered rude. Don't put them down in a crossed position, since that's supposed to bring bad luck.

Also, don't add salt or any other seasoning to your food. To the Chinese, that means you're telling them that the food wasn't prepared well.

Be careful how much you eat or drink. While there's no reason for you to leave the table still hungry, the Chinese consider it extremely bad taste for anyone to overdo it in eating and drinking.

The Chinese don't have refrigerators. But they have many ways of safely storing and preserving food. They can dry or smoke meat, salt fish, and pickle both meats and vegetables. This means that if you are in Chang'an and suddenly have a hunger for a crunchy pickle, you'll probably be able to find one.

The drink of choice in China is tea. It's properly drunk just as it is brewed, without adding sugar or milk. There are many different varieties of tea. Jasmine, a type that is still served in modern Chinese restaurants, has dried jasmine flowers in it. If you experiment, you're sure to soon find one or more teas that you like.

You'll probably want to do as the locals do and boil any water before drinking it, just in case of germs. There's no such thing as bottled water in ancient China, and there are no water purification plants, so you never can be quite sure how safe the water is.

TAKE IT from a Local

Never stick your chopsticks straight down into the rice. If you do, you'll be reminding everyone of funeral rituals, and you really don't want to do that!

WHERE TO
FIND SOUVENIRS

Goldsmiths made this pair of gilt leopards, inlaid with silver and garnets, that were used to weigh down the clothes of a deceased person. They were found in the tomb of Princess Tou Wan from the western lands of the Han dynasty.

ARTS, CRAFTS, & OTHER DELIGHTS

As you explore Chang'an or other Chinese cities, you are sure to come across squares where artisans have their shops. In these stores, you'll be able to find ceramics, jewelry, or beautiful carvings in smooth green or rare and expensive white jade.

If you visit any of Chang'an's marketplaces or shops, you will find artists painting beautiful scenes on silk scrolls. Other artists worth watching are goldsmiths crafting intricate and delicate gold ornaments or potters creating lovely glazed pottery with paintings of mountains and clouds, tigers, elephants, and even fantastic dragons.

BEST BUYS IN ANCIENT CHINA

- **Lacquer bowls and plates** (*right*)
- **Silk robes and slippers**
- **Embroidered robes and vests**
- **Jade amulets and sculptures**
- **Porcelain bowls and vases**
- **Writing brushes**
- **Calligraphic or painted scrolls**

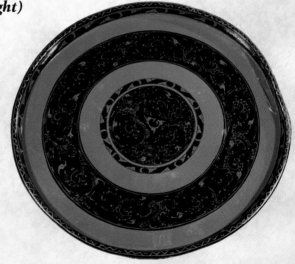

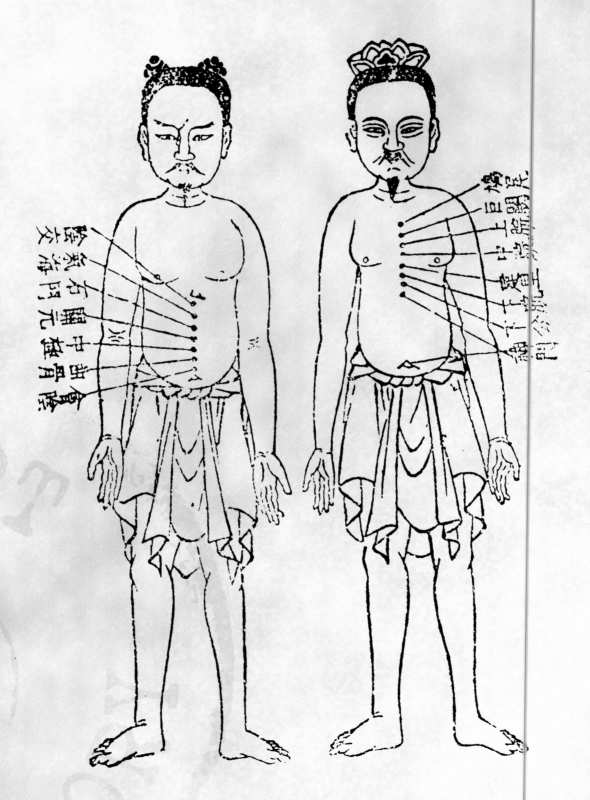

How to Stay Safe & Healthy

Take Some Ginseng and Call Me in the Morning

If you happen to get sick while visiting ancient China, don't worry. Chinese doctors are very skillful and well educated. By the time of the Han dynasty, several good medical guides have been compiled. One of the best known of these is the *Nei Jing,* or *Inner Canon,* which is an encyclopedia of Chinese medical knowledge. A new work called *Shang Han Lun,* the *Treatise on Diseases Caused by Cold Factors,* compiled by Doctor Zhang Zhongjing, adds more modern knowledge. Most doctors will have copies of both books.

By "cold factors," by the way, the Chinese don't mean the common cold. They believe that all diseases can be categorized as "cold" or "hot." They also believe in what we call holistic medicine. You don't just treat the illness, you treat the problem—which they call an imbalance—that has caused the disease.

When you go to a Chinese doctor, he'll usually follow several steps. First he'll ask about your symptoms and family history. After that, he'll give you a thorough exam, listening to your breathing as well as checking for any strange odors. Last, he'll check your pulse. Then he may prescribe an herbal remedy, such as ginseng, or acupuncture treatments or both.

Acupuncture

You may already know about acupuncture, since it's used in the modern world as well as in ancient China. But the treatment was developed in China. Acupuncture is the method of placing thin needles painlessly into specific points on the body through which the body's energy is

This acupuncture chart is from the Song dynasty (A.D. 960–1279). It shows acupuncture points that have been used by acupuncturists for centuries.

believed to flow. How it works is still a mystery, but acupuncture is used to relieve pain and help heal many types of injuries and disease. Acupuncture can also be used as a type of local anesthesia.

EXERCISE

When you're having fun on vacation, it's easy to forget to take good care of yourself. After all, there are so many new things to see, do, and eat that it seems a waste to spend time in exercise. But the followers of the Confucian way, who are likely to include many of ancient China's doctors, believe that your body is a gift from your parents. They believe that it would be wrong and downright rude of you not to take care of it. This means, of course, that everyone is expected to do his or her best to keep fit. If you have any doubts about what you should be doing, you can find good lists of exercises in any doctor's office.

HOLD ONTO YOUR WALLET

The poorer sections of large cities such as Chang'an can be dangerous for the unwary tourist. Fake fortunetellers may try to trick you out of your money, and thieves may attack and rob you.

Chang'an also has a problem with teen gangs. Each gang has its own special clothing, its special uniform. One gang might wear green tunics. Another might have red turbans. The teens wander the streets at night in search of danger and trouble, looking for rival gangs to fight or unwary tourists to rob. Since guards can't be everywhere at once in such a large a city, the wise tourist doesn't go out alone at night.

If you plan on doing any long-range travel in China, stay away from the borders. Emperor Wu Di is in the middle of an expansion of China's lands, as he also battles to control dangerous nomadic tribes at the borders. You might well find yourself caught up in a border dispute involving swords and arrows!

LAW AND ORDER

As a tourist, you may be wondering about public safety. What about those street gangs of teens in Chang'an? Do you need to keep a hand on your string of cash at all times? What happens if you do get robbed?

Yes, there is crime in ancient China. But if you take the ordinary care you would take when visiting any strange city, you'll do fine.

But even if something does happen to you, you can rest assured that ancient China in the Han dynasty has a very good system of law and order. The law books of the land are called the *Nine Chapters*. There are more than 906 books in the series. More than sixty legal subjects are covered, from robbery to reasons for arrest. These books are constantly updated with new cases and decisions. With these books, the Chinese courts can handle any situation.

Much of this terrific law system is due to Emperor Wu Di's prime minister, Dong Zhongshu. He is a wise man who follows the teachings of Confucius. Dong Zhongshu revised the code of law so that each person is considered equally important in the eyes of the law. Dong Zhongshu also has insisted that every law include an explanation. This means that there are no longer silly or pointless laws in the courts.

Some of Dong Zhongshu's changes in the law code include those concerning the rights of slaves. No longer can a slave owner kill a slave on a cruel whim. There are several cases in the law books of slave owners being punished. There is even one case of a slave owner who had killed one of his slaves and was forced to take his own life.

There are also laws protecting homeowners. Officials cannot break into someone's house or arrest someone without due cause. If a homeowner injures a thief who's broken in, the homeowner can't be sued.

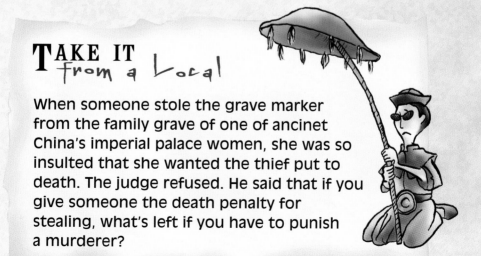

TAKE IT from a Local

When someone stole the grave marker from the family grave of one of ancinet China's imperial palace women, she was so insulted that she wanted the thief put to death. The judge refused. He said that if you give someone the death penalty for stealing, what's left if you have to punish a murderer?

WHO'S WHO IN ANCIENT CHINA

BAN ZHAO

Ban Zhao (ca. A.D. 45–116) is the foremost female Confucian of the Han dynasty. She is the imperial historian for the emperor Han Hedi, who rules from 88–105. Sister of the court historian Ban Gum, who dies in 92, she completes his important history, the *Han Annals.* Ban Zhao also serves as an adviser on state matters to the empress Deng. The empress becomes royal regent (leader) in 106. Ban Zhao is best known for her *Nu Jie,* or *Lessons for Women,* a set of Confucian moral guidelines for women.

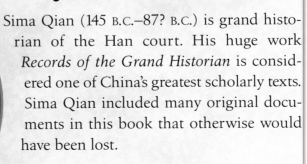

DONG ZHONGSHU

Dong Zhonshu (ca. first century B.C.) is prime minister to Emperor Wu Di and a follower of the teachings of Confucius. He revised the law code to honor the value of the individual. He also made it a crime to kill a slave.

SIMA QIAN

Sima Qian (145 B.C.–87? B.C.) is grand historian of the Han court. His huge work *Records of the Grand Historian* is considered one of China's greatest scholarly texts. Sima Qian included many original documents in this book that otherwise would have been lost.

WU DI

Wu Di (157 B.C.–87 B.C.) is a Han emperor noted both for his skill in military matters and for his love of learning and the arts. He created public schools in China and founded a university dedicated to the principles of Confucius.

ZHANG ZHEN

Zhang Zhen (?–114 B.C.), commander of the guards at Emperor Wu Di's imperial palace, volunteered in 138 B.C. to undertake a perilous journey to the west, where he found the famed Ferganian horses, the Heavenly Horses, and brought them back to China.

ZHANG ZHONGJING

Zhang Zhongjing (A.D. 168–196) is considered one of the great physicians of the Han dynasty. His most famous book is the *Shang Han Lun (Treatise on Diseases Caused by Colds Factors)* and is thought to be one of the best manuals of Chinese medicine ever written.

Preparing for the Trip

Make Your Own Scroll

You will need:

- 1 rectangular piece of smooth, solid-colored cotton fabric
- 1 rectangular piece of construction paper, two to three inches longer and wider than the silk
- fabric glue, such as Elmer's Fabric and Paper Glue, available at craft stores
- 1 pencil
- Acrylic paint and brushes or paint pens (the sort used to draw designs on fabric, not watercolors)
- 1 ribbon or ornamental cord

Glue the fabric to the construction paper, making sure that it doesn't wrinkle. Sketch a design very lightly on the fabric with the pencil. With the paint and brushes or the paint pens, paint in your design, letter, or poem. Let the paint dry for a day.

Once the painted fabric has fully dried, you can roll up your scroll and tie it with the ribbon or cord. If you want to hang the scroll, unroll it and tape the ribbon or cord to either end of the scroll. Loop the ribbon or cord over a nail.

Yangshao culture and the earliest signs of agriculture
5000–2700 B.C.

The Xia dynasty, the first Chinese dynasty
2205–1818 B.C.

Zhou dynasty and the rise of Confucianism and Taoism
1027–256 B.C.

5000 B.C.　　4000 B.C.　　3000 B.C.　　2000 B.C.　　1000 B.C.

The Longsham culture and the first domesticated animals in China
3500–2000 B.C.

The Shang dynasty, master bronze workers
1523–1027 B.C.

72

SZECHUAN CHICKEN

This recipe requires chopping and cooking over high heat, so you may want to ask an adult to help.

    4 boneless, skinless chicken breasts
    3 tablespoons cornstarch
    1 tablespoon vegetable oil
    3 cloves garlic chopped
    5 tablespoons soy sauce (You can use low calorie or low
        salt if you want)
    1 1/2 tablespoons white wine vinegar
    1 teaspoon sugar
    1/4 cup water
    6 green onions, cut into 1-inch pieces
    1/8 tablespoon cayenne pepper

Rinse the chicken in cool water. Cut the chicken into bite-sized pieces. Be sure to wash your hands and all your utensils after handling the chicken. Put the chicken cubes and cornstarch into a large plastic bag and shake until the cubes are coated.

Heat the oil in a skillet or wok. Add the chicken and garlic to the hot oil and stir them over medium-high heat until the chicken is lightly browned, about eight minutes. Meanwhile, in a small bowl, combine the soy sauce, vinegar, sugar, and water. Add to the pan. Cover and cook for three minutes, or until chicken is cooked through and does not show any pink in the middle. Add the green onions and cayenne to the mix and cook the meal uncovered about two minutes more. Serve with rice. *(Serves 4)*

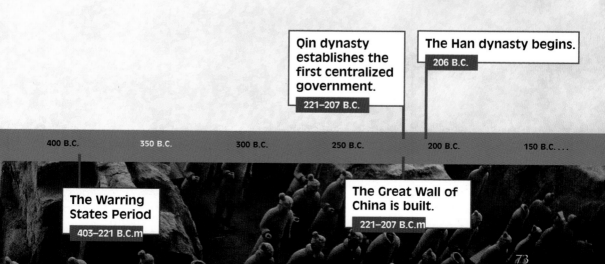

Qin dynasty establishes the first centralized government.
221–207 B.C.

The Han dynasty begins.
206 B.C.

400 B.C.   350 B.C.   300 B.C.   250 B.C.   200 B.C.   150 B.C. . . .

The Warring States Period
403–221 B.C.m

The Great Wall of China is built.
221–207 B.C.m

GLOSSARY

amulet: an object worn to ward off evil

calligraphy: the art of producing artistic, stylized, elegant handwriting

dynasty: a family that rules for several generations

Heavenly Horses: the name given by the emperor Wu Di to the horses brought east to China from Fergana

jade: a smooth, glossy stone that comes in shades from dark green to white

lacquer: a glossy substance, like resin from pine trees, used to coat pots, trays, and ornaments

nomads: a group of people who wander with their herds, usually according to the seasons, in search of food and water

porcelain: a fine, white form of ceramic

silk: a smooth, fine fabric spun from the threads of silkworm cocoons

terra-cotta: a hard, waterproof ceramic often used in buildings and statues

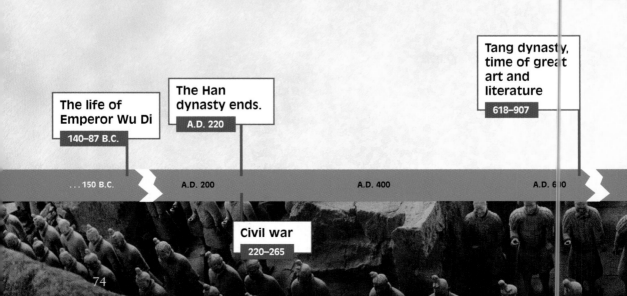

The life of Emperor Wu Di
140–87 B.C.

The Han dynasty ends.
A.D. 220

Tang dynasty, time of great art and literature
618–907

. . . 150 B.C.   A.D. 200   A.D. 400   A.D. 600

Civil war
220–265

Pronunciation Guide

Ban Gum	BAHN GOOM
Ban Zhao	BAHN JOW
Chang'an	JAHNG ahn
Chang Ch'ian	jahng JEE'ehn
Chang Chung-ching	jahng JUNG-jeeng
Ching ming	JEENG MEENG
Dong Zhongshu	dong JOON-shoo
Dunhuang	doon-HWAHNG
fai jee	FY JEE
Guan Yin	GWAHN YEEN
Han Hedi	HAHN HAY-dee
Jiadoi	JY-DOY
Kashgar	KAHSH-gahr
K'ung Fu-tzu	KONG FOOD-zoo
Liu Pang	LEEYOO BAHNG
Luoyang	lwoh-YAHNG
Ma Yuan	mah YOO-wahn
Nei Ching	NAY CHIHNG
Nu Jie	NOO JEE-yeh
Qin Shi Huangdi	CHIHN SHIR HWAHNG-dee
Shang Han Lun	SHAHNG HAHN LOON
Shen Nung	SHEHN NOONG
Sima Qian	SEE-mah CHEEN
Wen Chang	WEHN CHAHNG
Wu Di	WOO DEE
Xiongnu	SHEE-uhng-noo
Xuan Wu	SHOO-AHN WOO
Yumen Guan	YOO-mehn GWAHN

Yuan dynasty, ruled by Mongol leader Kublai Khan
1280–1367

Qing (Manchu), last dynasty
1644–1911

The People's Republic of China is founded.
1949

1200   1400   1600   1800   2000

Ming dynasty
1368–1644

Republic of China
1911–1949

FURTHER READING

Books

Baldwin, Robert F. *Daily Life in Ancient and Modern Beijing*. Minneapolis: Lerner Publications Company, 1999.

Cotterell, Arthur. *Ancient China*. London and New York: DK Publishing, 2000.

DuTemple, Leslie. *The Great Wall of China*. Minneapolis: Lerner Publications Company, 2003.

Immell, Myra. *Han Dynasty*. San Diego, CA: Lucent Books, 2002.

Rees, Rosemary. *Ancient Chinese: Understanding People from the Past*. Chicago: Heinemann, 2002.

Shuter, Jane. *The Ancient Chinese*. Chicago: Heinemann, 1997.

Teague, Ken. *Growing Up in Ancient China*. Mahwah, NJ: Troll, 1993.

Internet Sites

"China from 1200 B.C. to 221 B.C." *EMuseum*. Minnesota State University at Mankato. n.d.
<http://emuseum.mankato.msus.edu/prehistory/china/> (August 13, 2003).

Donn, Lin, and Don Donn. *Daily Life in Ancient China*. October 23, 2002 .
<http://members.aol.com/Donnclass/Chinalife.html> (August 13, 2003).

Grimes, Karah L. "The Emperor Wu Ti." *North Park University*. December 11, 1996.
<http://www.campus.northpark.edu/history/WebChron/China/WuTi.html> (August 13, 2003).

Hooker, Richard. "Ancient China: The Middle Kingdom." *Washington State University: World Civilizations*. 1996.
<http://www.wsu.edu:8080/~dee/ANCCHINA/ANCCHINA.HTM> (August 13, 2003).

Ross, Kelley E. "Confucius." *The Proceedings of the Friesian School*. 2003.
<http://www.friesian.com/confuci.htm> (August 13, 2003)

BIBLIOGRAPHY

Ban, Gu. *Courtier and Commoner in Ancient China: Selections from the History of the Former Han.* Translated by Burton Watson. New York: Columbia University Press, 1974.

Beinfield, Harriet, and Efrem Korngold. *Between Heaven and Earth: A Guide to Chinese Medicine.* New York: Ballantine Books, 1992.

Birrell, Anne. *Popular Songs and Ballads of Han China.* Honolulu: University of Hawaii Press, 1993.

Cotterell, Arthur. *Ancient China.* London and New York: DK Publishing, 2000.

Eberhard, Wolfram. *A Dictionary of Chinese Symbols.* London and New York: Routledge & Kegan Paul Ltd., 1986.

Ebrey, Patricia Buckley, ed. *Chinese Civilization: A Sourcebook.* New York: The Free Press, 1996.

Eichhorn, Werner. *Chinese Civilization: An Introduction.* Translated by Janet Seligman. London: Faber and Faber, 1969.

Goscoigne, Bamber. *The Dynasties and Treasures of China.* New York: The Viking Press, 1973.

Hucker, Charles O. *China's Imperial Past: An Introduction to Chinese History and Culture.* Stanford, CA: Stanford University Press, 1975.

Loewe, Michael. *Everyday Life in Early Imperial China: During the Han Period 202 B.C.–A.D. 220.* New York: G. P. Putnam's Sons, 1968.

Michaelson, Carol, ed. *Ancient China.* Sydney and San Francisco: Time-Life Books, 1996.

Morton, W. Scott. *China: Its History and Culture.* New York: McGraw-Hill, 1982.

Paludan, Ann. *Chronicle of the Chinese Emperors: The Reign-by-Reign Record of the Rulers of Imperial China.* London and New York: Thames and Hudson, 1998.

Schloss, Ezekiel. *Art of the Han.* New York: China Institute, 1979.

Sima Quan. *Records of the Grand Historian: Han Dynasty I.* Vol. 1. Translated by Burton Watson. New York: Columbia University Press, 1993.

T'Ung-Tsu Ch'u. *Han Social Structure.* Seattle: University of Washington Press, 1972.

Waley, Arthur. *Three Ways of Thought in Ancient China.* London: George Allen & Unwin Ltd., 1939.

INDEX

ABOUT THE AUTHOR

Josepha Sherman is a professional author, folklorist, and editor. A former assistant curator for the Metropolitan Museum of Art in New York City, she has a degree in Ancient Near Eastern Archaeology. Among her titles for younger readers are *Your Travel Guide to Ancient Israel, Bill Gates: Computer King, Deep Space Observational Satellites, Welcome to the Rodeo*, and numerous others. She is a winner of the Compton Crook Award for best first fantasy novel and has been nominated numerous times for the Nebula Award. She lives in New York City.

Acknowledgments for Quoted Material p. 24, Ma Yuan quoted in "Monks and Merchants/Heavenly Horses and the Aftermath of Empire." *Asia Society,* n.d. <http://www.asiasociety.org/arts/monksandmerchants/horses.htm> (August 13, 2003); p. 39, *The Prentice-Hall Encyclopedia of World Proverbs,* edited by Wolfgang Mieder (Englewood Cliffs, NJ: Prentice-Hall, 1989); p. 41, *Confucius: The Analects,* translated by D. C. Lau (New York: Penguin, 1998); p. 55, *Confucius: The Analects,* translated by D. C. Lau (New York: Penguin, 1998).

Photo Acknowledgments
The images in this book are used with the permission of:
© The Art Archive/Genius of China Exhibition/The Art Archive, pp. 2, 24, 64, 65 (top); © Billy Hustace, pp. 6–7; © Erich Lessing/Art Resource, NY, pp. 8–9, 32–33; © Keren Su/CORBIS, p. 12; © Galen Rowell/CORBIS, p. 14; © China Stock, pp. 15, 23 (bottom), 26 (©Liu Liqun), 66, 70 (both), 71 (both); © Snark/Art Resource, NY, p. 17; © Réunion des Musées Nationaux/Art Resource, NY, p. 19; from The Alphabet Makers, courtesy Museum of the Alphabet, p. 20; Cultural Relics Publishing House, Beijing, p. 21; © Werner Forman/Art Resource, NY, pp. 22, 28 (bottom); © Giraudon/Art Resource, NY, pp. 23 (top), 31, 57; © Royal Ontario Museum/CORBIS, pp. 27, 28 (top), 48, 54 (bottom), 56; © Lowell Georgia/CORBIS, p. 30; © The Art Archive/Musée Cernuschi Paris/Dagli Orti, pp. 36, 39, 60; © Asian Art & Archaeology, Inc./CORBIS, pp. 38, 45, 51, 54 (top), 65 (bottom); California Academy of Sciences, p. 41; © The British Museum, p. 42; © The Art Archive/Dagli Orti, p. 47; © Bettmann/CORBIS, p. 50 (top); © Werner Forman/CORBIS, p. 50 (bottom); © Liang Zhuoming/CORBIS, p. 53; © Mark Anderson, p. 59; © Royalty-Free/CORBIS, p. 62; © The Art Archive, pp. 72–73, 74–75; Maps by Laura Westlund, pp. 10–11, 34–35; Cartoons by Tim Parlin.

Front cover: © Asian Art & Archaeology, Inc./CORBIS (top); © Burstein Collection/CORBIS (bottom).